Don't Have Sex 9 Months Before Christmas and Other Practical Financial Tips

RoseMarie Keogh-Smyth

LUCKY BOOK PUBLISHING

Published by Lucky Book Publishing:
www.luckybookpublishing.com

Paperback ISBN: 978-1-998287-43-7
E-book ISBN: 978-1-998287-42-0

Cover Art by Chloe Adams, for more information:
www.artofchadams.com

1st edition, November 2024.

“The definition of ‘insanity’ is doing the same thing over and over again and expecting different results.”

- Albert Einstein

Ready for change?

To your Sweeping success,

Ray

My Gift To You

As a special thank you for reading,
get FREE Access to the book resources.

Scan the QR Code below or visiting
https://www.mortgagelessmentor.ca/
bookresources

Dedication

I dedicate this book to my grandmother, Kathleen Llewellyn Chapman, a.k.a. Little Ga. As I write the dedication, she is 99 years old and still living in her own home. I thank you, Little Ga, for passing on your financial sense gene. If I had to choose between two of your incredible skills, finance and gardening, I am quite happy with my black thumb.

Thank you to my first love, my husband Todd Smyth, who, very early in Round Two of our relationship, recognized my skill with money and stepped back to let me run the household finances. He still symbolically hands me the pay stubs - and the bills!

To our son who wants it all, and wants it now: May my voice always be there to guide your adult years, and may you continue to save for big and glorious goals. I cannot wait to see your first car! It is the one savings goal you have stayed faithful to since you were six years old.

To all my friends and the Keogh Clan who support this wild and crazy life of mine with walking, talking and laughter: I would not shine as brightly nor entertain you half as much without your support and friendship.

Forewarning

“Everything can’t be a priority at the same time”
-Jo Bendle, Creator of the Meant for More® Method

You are going to read a lot of tips in this book and discover many best practices you can implement. But you can’t do everything at once. It will take time. And that’s ok. Please don’t read chapter after chapter and think: where am I getting the money to do all this? Focus on the topics that will make the biggest impact in your life. Kick the debt and save some; in time you will be able to save a lot! As you work towards a brighter financial future, celebrate your efforts. Do **not** go into debt on these celebrations! Many are free. Major milestones, however, deserve major celebrations.

Give yourself permission to write in this book. I can hear some of you scream in pain: I hear you! I LOVE books. Generally, if you dog-ear, write in or crack the spine on one of my books, you will never borrow another book from my library again. But in this case, your financial future is more important than keeping this book in pristine condition. Use it as a workbook! Here are some of the things you might check off:

- ☐ Debt Cleared
- ☐ Down payment saved
- ☐ Dream Achieved
- ☐ Mortgage Paid
- ☐ Insurance, wills and power of attorney in place
- ☐ Education Fund
- ☐ Emergency Fund
- ☐ F.U. Account (thank you for this, Gail Vaz-Oxlade!)
- ☐ Monitor the credit rating
- ☐ Best Fit, not best priced decisions

For those of you like me, who still just cannot deface a book, I will provide some printables on my website: www.MortgagelessMentor.ca/BookResources

For the rest of you: save paper and scribble away!!

Contents

Preface

Are you tired of living paycheque to paycheque, knowing you can do better? Tired of interest rates and late fees? Dreaming of a bigger life - and at the same time scared of what your retirement will look like? Are you putting off insurance and writing a will due to discomfort?

Now is the right time to finally take care of your finances!

Welcome to a moment in time where your dreams and a plan come together - in the form of big decisions, protection and investments tailored to meet the needs of your future self and your family.

By the end of this book, you will be using the money you are already spending on debt and savings in the best possible way to achieve financial freedom. You will be "finding" money you didn't know you had and using it to great effect. You will be giggling as you pay off your debt and watch your savings grow.

I urge you to embrace my dad's philosophy: 'I'll try anything once, and if it doesn't kill me, I might even try it again!' I've joyfully lived by this, welcoming adventure and summoning the courage to try what seems impossible—because, let's face it, if what I'm doing isn't working, why not try something new? If you're reading this book, what you're doing isn't working. So try it! It might just save you.

For those of you who only read this book and do not do one single action I recommend, you will, at least once, curse my name as I ruin an automatic purchase and wonder if there really is a better way. Is this coffee or pair of shoes going to give you more joy in this moment than achieving your biggest dream in three to five years? If so: Charge! If not, you may be slower to tap. With continued purchasing patterns that bury you in debt, my voice will fade from your brain. I promise.

I'm Rosy "the Mortgageless Mentor" and I want to address the action-takers looking to achieve more, be it home ownership, deep savings accounts, mortgage freedom, retirement accounts or freedom of any kind - those who are interested in building a rock-solid future while still living in the moment.

I am here to lead the charge on changing the way we think about money management, debt and savings.

I refuse to accept that we cannot live a full life while paying down debt AND saving for the future. I believe in the one-two punch of paying debt and increasing savings to keep you on target and excited about what is to come.

Why should you listen to me anyway (you may ask)?

Because I walk the walk. And sometimes I stumble, just like you.

In the 4.5 years it took me to pay off my student loans, I bought my Harley, put 10% down on a condo and started paying my uncle and aunt in instalments for a piece of land on the water. These were big dreams, amazing opportunities that far outweighed a new pair of shoes. Since then, I bought my perfect home followed by rental homes for amazing families to settle in, heal and be safe. I took a solo dream vacation to Ireland, met my nephew and his family in Disney for Christmas, my entire family started racing BMX across the province, and I accomplished my most coveted achievement: Mortgage Freedom.

I don't say this to brag or to say I am special. I worked, as you do. I think the only difference between me and the person with the 45-year-old student loan was my stubborn defiance about letting my money go coupled with the ability to focus on one debt with ferocity and one dream that was massive in my eyes - and heart. That one-two punch of Debt and Dream.

So ask yourself two questions:

1. What debt, if paid off, would be life changing?
2. What dream would far outweigh daily purchases, emotional shopping and bored scrolling?

List a few ideas here:

Great - now you've got these, keep them in mind as we move through the rest of the book

The Essentials

**“The first essentials, of course,
is to know what you want”
- Robert Collier**

Budgets are Bullshit

Didn’t expect that, now did you? Usually, at this point in a finance book, you are reading once again that you need to pull out six months of spending habits and enter them into an excel sheet to figure out your actuals, compare your wants vs. needs list, use pivot tables, prepare a powerpoint presentation and finally, print off a Perfect Budget to live by. Have you done it yet? Or is that when the book went into the bin or was wrapped up for a “friend”?

As Warren Buffet says, “Do not save what is left after spending, but spend what is left after saving.”[1]

---

1 Warren Buffett, “Do not save what is left after spending, but spend what is left after saving,” Quotlr, accessed, 4 October, 2024, https://quotlr.com/author/warren-buffett.

Yes, you need to know how much income is coming into the house. Yes, you need to know how much it costs to keep the lights on and to not lose your house to taxes. No, you do not need to know that you will be spending $143.49 at the grocery store this week.

So, here's a quick exercise:

On payday, we receive this amount
in our accounts: $___________

We receive this many paycheques
a year: x___________

In one year, our family has this to
cover our lives $___________

I solemnly promise not to spend more than this amount on needs, wants and investments.

Sign Here: ______________________________

Debt is not a Postal Code!!

We are not meant to spend our lives digging out of bad decisions, broken relationships, market crashes, mortgage rate spikes and generational poverty. No one needs to move in and settle into debt. It is a temporary measure caused by accident or choice, sometimes disastrously fast, sometimes slowly, tap by tap.

When you were two and you covered your eyes, you thought you were invisible. You disappeared and no one could see you! As you grew, you realized the truth. The same is true for debts. Just because you cover your eyes, it does not mean you or your debt disappears.

I moved out when I was 16 years old. I paid bills, finished high school and went to university. And immediately went into debt. My student loans were high, and I made poor choices on the needs vs. wants list: the items I *needed* to survive and the items I *wanted*, like drinks with friends, a guitar and more books I had no time to read. While books are often placed on the "needs" side - my friend, Jamie Dodd, and I designed a week-long road trip to the U.S. around a Woodstock bookstore visit with our children in the summer of 2024 - common sense must be applied to even our healthy addictions! At that debt-ridden time in my life, however, there was a bit of a feeling that I was so far in debt, so what did this one purchase matter? Others were further in debt than me, right? And it didn't hurt. There was no cost. Until there was...

One day, school was over and student loans were due. And there was interest!! Legend has it I broke out in hives at the sight of my bill. How much money did they want? Of MINE?!? Conveniently forgetting that I had been living on their dime for 4.5 years, of course.

After freaking out - just a bit - I thought: no way am I going to do this forever, be 60 and still paying my student loans. So I made a decision: it took me 4.5 years to get in debt - it would take me 4.5 years to get out. Whatever the cause of debt, determination is required now. Do not stay in the space of vulnerability and need - breathe, make a plan and do NOT get distracted by shiny things. Decide that this is not permanent. Decide that you are deserving and entitled to live a debt-free life. Make it personal! That debt stands between you and

Easy Street. It sucks up money you could happily spend on better things. Look at the number and say:

"You're going *down*!!"

Start with a Credit Check

Have you ever opened a credit card, used it for a few years and thought you cancelled it? Applied for a credit card to get a baseball cap or t-shirt? Thought you removed someone from your credit card or bank account access? Run away from a cell phone company, swearing never to pay them that outrageous charge you never incurred? Failed to close an old bank account? Co-signed for a friend or family member? Returned a vehicle and not read the fine print on owing the difference between the auction price and your debt?

Any of these things can come back to haunt you when you least expect it - and when you really don't have extra time or money to deal with clearing up an old mistake. Maybe one you didn't even know you made.

I have a friend, Reagan, who, after 17 years of renting, had his landlady walk in and say, "I'm selling. The real estate agent will be here Monday to appraise and list the house." He lives four doors from work, has a beekeeping business on his property and provides a safe house of pizza pops for the local high school kids, his junior firefighter squad. And the house is going on the market? Can you say *stress*??

During our conversation, I refer him to a mortgage broker, and he makes the sound decision to get approved for a mortgage and starts the painful process. Keep in mind, a good mortgage broker can make this easier, but no matter how good they are, you still have a lot of paperwork to find and provide. Seems to be different every time I buy a house!

He hasn't paid attention to his credit score as he thought all was well and he has never needed more than he had. Much to his surprise, there was a significant debt in collections he had never heard about. Seems when he thought he was making a responsible decision of returning a vehicle that was beyond his means, due to unforeseen circumstances arising after purchase, they sold the vehicle at auction and he owed the difference: $24,000. The dealership didn't tell him and sent it to collections, who started sending mail to an old address.

He is on a timeline to get approved on a mortgage and is faced with a $24,000 debt that needs clearing before he can move forward. Are you starting to feel a little stressed as you read this? Think it can't happen to you? Maybe you should take a few minutes and check your score just in case.

For the curious, with a few extensions from an understanding landlady, he sealed the deal and now owns his own home. And yes, we celebrated!!

Your turn! Get that credit report and deal with whatever you may find. Re-check every year, just in case.

Don't Jump on the Debt Consolidation Train

Many people rack up the debts and think consolidation or reverse mortgages or other "easy button" approaches will save them. Often, after hiding the debt or running from it, people rack it up all over again! Even if they do learn from their error and don't fall back in debt, they are in financial jail for many years while their credit scores attempt to recover.

Face the debt, stop the spending, and pull yourself out. Admittedly, there are circumstances in which that is not possible, but I have witnessed so many who jump for the Debt Consolidation Life Raft too quickly. Luckily, I got to Ashley in time.

Ashley posted on Facebook seeking advice on her debt, which was overwhelming her mind and life. She was losing sleep and desperate to find a way out. So many people advised her to seek consolidation or a proposal. A friend of mine suggested that she have a conversation with me first. Immediately, I received a meeting request for that very afternoon, and I am so happy I was able to accommodate.

Within 45 minutes, I ran Ashley through some easy actions she could take that would have an immediate effect on her debt. We prioritised the debt, worked through weekly goals and planned exactly how she would maximize her upcoming backpay and her tax refund. We even planned the first celebration, the first $10,000 that represented a final closure to an old chapter of her life. She could finally be free of the emotional weight of a bad relationship attached to that debt! By the end of the call, she felt empowered and determined to overcome. The tips I shared are included in this book.

Time for a Plan!

**"Few people have any next,
they live from hand to mouth without a plan,
And are always at the end of their line."
- Ralph Waldo Emerson**

You are already paying a certain sum to your debts every month as you put a little more here and a little more there and try to keep the wolves from the door. That is why I am starting with debt, not the everyday spending. I want you to take what you are already putting into debt and make it more efficient. We will push the Easy Button on the daily expenses next.

With the attitude of an assassin, I want you to write out all the debts, the interest payments that eat into your savings, the personal cost of a sibling's or a parent's generous helping hand, the guilty hidden debt to a phone company or utility you are hiding from. We are going to adult hard, face the reality and blow these debts away, one by one.

Full List of Debts, No Hiding

Who do I owe?	How much do I owe?	Interest Charge (Financial & Emotional)	Amount I currently pay (Monthly or per paycheque)

Now that you see it all laid out, take a breath, maybe pour a stiff drink and come back to me when you are ready. I promise it will get easier. You just completed the hardest part.

You came back! Congratulations. We can do this. We are now going to prioritise the debts.

Keep in mind the highest interest rate may not be the highest cost. If you have borrowed from a friend or relative, and they are not charging you interest - even if they are! - you want to eliminate that debt and think up an equivalent thank you gesture or gift. Do not go into debt on a thank you, but consider what they had to do: decreasing their liquid assets or ability to borrow in order for you to have what you wanted. Return the favour, and make a sacrifice for them.

Maybe it is a debt from an unfinished degree that you are sick of thinking about or a former spouse you just want to delete from your memory banks - then line that debt up and fire away!

Caveat: no exes shall be harmed in the elimination of this debt!

The first debt to tackle is the one that costs the most. Is that emotional or financial? That is up to you. Pick one that, when paid, is going to have the biggest impact on you, personally. This has nothing to do with anyone but you. Got it? Write it at the top of the list.

And then you go for financial benefit. Debt #2 is the highest interest rate, followed by all debts in order of interest rate, highest to lowest. Credit card companies are open to phone calls, setting a plan in place and even lowering your interest rate to ensure they get their money. Ask! You may be pleasantly surprised and need to re-order this list once more. Once completed, print the debt list and post it on the fridge. Let your family in on the news that you are taking out your debt. Keep it front and centre. If you have children, this is a time they can perhaps learn from your mistakes instead of their own.

How much do you currently pay towards debts? $___________

How much is the minimum payment on all debts? $___________

The difference between these two numbers is $___________*

(*This number will go in column three of the chart below)

All debts on the list are paid at the minimum required to stay out of collections. You do not miss a payment; you do not redirect the money. This is important for your financial health and recovery. To ensure your success, set the payments up on auto pay - every payday, you automatically transfer the money from your account to the debt. Do not set an end date for this. It continues as long as there is debt, and as you pay things off, you will find joy in deleting that auto payment.

The rest of any money noted above, that you have already been directing to debt repayment, goes to the top debt, the evil debt, the debt that must be paid. Any "found" money - tax rebate, gifts, the tricks later in this book - they ALL go to this one debt. Later, we will add a dream, and you will see how you can build towards debt freedom and amazing dreams.

Remember my student loan debt? Well, once I'd decided to pay it off it was the single debt I focused on. When the bank told me I couldn't pay the student loan without an invoice, I made photocopies. If I had $20, I walked to my bank, Scotiabank, on my lunch break. I worked all the hours I used to work and study, mixing full time, part time and seasonal work, and I paid off my debt.

Once that debt is cleared, you celebrate! This doesn't give you permission to go back in debt, but a celebration needs to occur to solidify the importance in your brain. And to make you want to do it again! Have that fancy coffee, or a night on the dancefloor, or guilt-free Netflix binge! You earned it.

Before the next payday, delete the auto pay to the cleared debt and increase the auto pay on debt #2, which is now the top debt, the evil debt, the debt that must be paid! You have just increased your payments on the next debt and will quickly see the results. That debt is going to melt away. And when it is gone, you will celebrate and take all the money you were once paying on debt #1 and on debt #2 and aim it at debt #3. Do you see the cascading effect we are going to have on this debt? Can you feel the excitement yet? The endorphins rising? The celebrations you are going to be experiencing? Should we create a playlist now??

Debts in Order of Annoyance

Name that Debt	Minimum Payment Required to Avoid Collections	*Additional Amount Focused on Debt Annihilation (see number above)	How will I Celebrate When It Is GONE?
Most Annoying Debt:	$	$	
	$		
	$		
	$		
	$		
	$		
	$		
	$		
	$		
	$		

Automation

Running on autopilot can be uncomfortable, even scary - ever find yourself at work and not really remember the drive? Well, when it comes to finances, you can use it to your advantage!

How would this look if it were easy?

All the bills would be paid on time, meaning no late fees: savings rising, debt falling. Children's education funds would be paid. New dreams surfacing with plans for achieving them. Money would not be the reason for stress.

The first step to achieving all this is to set your paycheque on autopilot. You already created the list of annoying debts and automated them.

Now, to get your bills in order...

First, we need to make sure you don't run further into debt! List your bills - are they monthly, every other month, annual? Are they set or do they change every month?

Set up automatic payments for the next payday - this commitment to debt freedom will also help you tame your spending, as your bills will be paid before you wake up on payday and you will have a clear picture of your available spending.

Starting with the regular bills (same amount every month or every other month); break it down by the number of paycheques you receive between bills and set your payment to pay the same amount every payday. You owe $200 every other month and four paycheques to get there? $50 a paycheque and you can smile when the bill comes in, knowing you are covered. Always open and read the bill to ensure the payments are flowing and no change has occurred - and to enjoy the feeling of being ahead!!

Next come the irregular amounts: water bill, heating bill and credit cards for example. Estimate the bills knowing there will be major fluctuation in heating and cooling in extreme seasons. As you open the bills, you will see how well you estimated and can adjust as required.

For annual bills, you may need a separate account where each paycheque sends a portion of the money over so that it is there when you need it. This includes insurance, land taxes, licence renewal, professional fees, life insurance...

If you use your credit card to pay your bills, calculate the monthly amount and split it between your paycheques. Yes, you will get an extra payment every few months towards your purchases. Be sure to pay down your credit card in full every month to avoid snowballing back into debt on your highest interest bill.

For those of you who do not trust yourselves with a credit card, this is a great way to build your credit. Set up a few bills on the card and then cut it up. Instead of paying the individual bills you can lump it all together and send a set amount every payday to your credit card. The credit company will see activity and that you pay in full every month. If you really need to use a credit card for a big purchase such as going on vacation, you can call the credit card company and tell them your card was destroyed. They will ship a new one - you will use it and cut it up as soon as you get home from your travels.

A note to the entrepreneurs, real estate agents, mortgage brokers, coaches, finance advisers/advisors (though I truly hope you are using all your skills on your own lives and leading by example) and others whose income is not regular: you will need to figure out your annual expenses and manage that in chunks as invoices are paid. Automation will not work well for you as you do not know when the next deal will close. Meet with a financial adviser or advisor to discuss your particular needs. Live below your means to ensure financial security at all times. Invest in you, not in stuff. If you are still feeling jammed, focus on the sweep until you can wiggle loose (that gem of a tip is in the next section). When a debt is paid off, or a big bill is paid from the savings instead of the line of credit, you will know you are coming to the light.

Bill and Savings Goals

Name of bill/ savings goal	Frequency (ie monthly, annual)	Amount per pay	☑ when automated

Habits

"We are what we repeatedly do.
Excellence then is not an act, but a habit."
-Aristotle

Do you want to crank up your effectiveness with your money? This next little tip really packs a punch.

Sweep it Under the Rug

There are some who say I don't clean: I just clean with purpose. I sweep!

Every day, go to your online banking and sweep the "small change" into a specific account or onto one bill (pick one and commit). You can sweep the cents, the singles or the tens. Do this often enough, you will sweep hundreds and thousands. I swept the thousands once before publishing this book, and let me assure you: it felt amazing!!

When dealing with debt, you will notice that your interest payments are starting to be covered by the daily sweep, leaving your automated payment to tackle principal. By adding the little bits throughout the week to your debt, you will be closer to debt free! Try it **now**. Log into your bank account and sweep the singles and change to a specific account (a debt or a dream). If your balance is $1,235.37, sweep $5.37.

As you clean the accounts, notice that you don't miss the loose change. Increase the cleaning by a decimal place. If you were cleaning $1,235.37 to $1,230.00, move to the left by one, leaving $1,200 in the account. Instead of $5.37 on your debt, you just moved $35.37! If that hurts too much, move $25.37, bringing you to $1,210. The goal is to sweep the money until you feel a pinch, then ease off a little. Settle where you are not noticing the loss and absolutely noticing the gain!

Account	$ in account	Light Sweep	Power Sweep	365 Days of Sweeping
Chequing 1	$1,235.37	$0.37	$ 35.37	
Savings 1	$ 198.08	$0.08	$ 98.08	
Savings 2	$ 987.78	$0.78	$ 87.78	
New Sweep Account		$1.23	$221.23	$448.95 - $80,748.19

While I am not suggesting that you will be sweeping $81,000 next year, if you sweep daily you will have thousands available to you that you didn't even notice before.

How much did you sweep today? $

What time are you sweeping tomorrow?

Pop a reminder into your calendar or set an alarm to sweep daily!

They Call Him the Streak[2]

We all love a good streak! The more often we do something, the more likely we are to keep going. Think of joining the gym or going on a daily walk. That first time is HARD - and the second is sometimes harder. But it is so much easier with friends. My neighbour, Trina, and I walk almost every weekday, no matter if we are melting or freezing. Canadian weather is all over the place. We go out around 7:20 a.m., meet up on the street like a couple of school girls and walk anywhere from one hour to half the day if we have a day off and the conversation is zingy. It is great for my shape as well as my mind! But if it weren't for Trina, would I still be walking even though I know how good it is for me? Trina says I never say no to a walk: I don't want to let her down as I know walking is her favourite form of down time and I feel so much better afterwards. We are both so incredibly grateful to have each other in our lives and on these walks! So we show up for each other. The Sweep will be the same for you! You can do it over coffee, or walks, or talks, or on a video call; you don't even have to be in

2 Stevens, Ray, "The Streak", Boogity Boogity Album, Barnaby Records, 1974

the same country. Share your dream and your debt annihilation date, and then each day, how much you swept. Keep each other motivated. Change each other's lives. Added bonus: you keep in touch!

I want you to set a goal to go four weeks sweeping daily with a friend. Now set a scheduler in both your calendars at the same time every day to connect and check your accounts. See it as a gift to yourself, your future and your friendship.

You may not sweep every day - if you do, you may have a shopping problem! - but the daily check in is what you are aiming for.

'Twas the Night Before Payday

Each payday is another opportunity to choose how you will spend your hard earned money. Some will treat themselves til there is nothing left in the account, thinking *I deserve this.... and this, and this, and this*. Some will pay the bills and spend the rest. Some won't even think and simply see what happens, never thinking a day will come when there is no income. We work forever, right?

The night before the next payday, take a breath. Consider where you are and where you want to be by the end of the year, a year from now, in five years, at the end of the decade. What bills, if paid off, will be life-changing? That car payment—gone. The interest on the credit card—now yours. The mortgage: paid.

Be brave and push some of your hard-earned money to something impactful. Invest it in a way that will make a difference. You picked one debt and one dream earlier. Lock in. Whatever is left in the account today is split 50/50 between the two and set a transfer up for tomorrow - never let your account ride at $0. Tomorrow, when you see your brand new paycheque, send 5% to each. Make some changes today and reap the rewards forever.

Action Item: Put a reminder in your calendar to go to your online banking the night before payday for the next five years. Better yet, click on no end date on the recurring event. Set up the two transfers for the next day - Dream, Debt. Know that tomorrow you will be closer to your dreams.

Bonuses, Taxes and Gifts, Oh My!

Everyone gets excited when "extra money" comes in! Whether it's a bonus at work, a tax refund, a birthday card from your grandmother or that three-pay month that everyone celebrates - endorphin levels rise and sugarplums and shopping dance in our heads.

Yes, you could go shopping. You could go out to eat. You could buy and buy and buy.

Or you could pause. Take a moment and once again picture what debt freedom looks like. What a full emergency fund looks like. What achieving a dream would feel like. What it would feel like to have money invested with no other purpose than to open doors, to allow possibilities, to accept an opportunity to do what you have always dreamed of doing.

To really launch you into a new mindset, take that money and make it count! Before the money enters your hands, have the one place that would truly make a difference already firmly in mind. Get excited about what it will mean for you. That dinner or fancy coffee - where will that be in a year? That new shirt, new boots, new whatever? You can work that into the budget and save up for it if you need it. But this money...THIS money is magic. Times like this can make all the difference.

Magical Money Goes Here	

This can be your number one debt or dream identified earlier, or maybe there is a deeper desire that no one else knows about. Give it a nickname if you are not yet ready to reveal it to the world.

Pay off Your Mortgage

"The paid-off home mortgage has taken the place of the BMW as the status symbol of choice."
-Dave Ramsey

There is a video available at mortgagelessmentor.ca/mortgagefree.

While I wish more people agreed with Dave Ramsay, I do know that you can pay off your mortgage sooner than the bank says you can. How do I know? Because I did it, and you and I are not that different.

Whether you're sick and tired of seeing all that interest go to the bank or you've been knocking debts down one at a time. Maybe this is the only debt you can exert control over. I know when it seemed that something was always breaking or going sideways, the only payment that I could make that wasn't coming back next month was my mortgage! Whatever the reason, it is time to take it down.

Yet, you also need to live this life that you have created and do not want to be paying every penny to the mortgage. While I could have achieved mortgage freedom a few years earlier than I did, I would never trade the memories I made in those years, both with family (on trips, during outings and through sports we joined) and solo on my month-long odyssey to Ireland in 2017.

The great thing about knowing exactly what you want out of life is that you can easily say no to the distractions, leaving your resources for what matters.

Know this: A mortgage is NOT a life sentence!!!

ALSO: Your mortgage is NOT a credit card! When you roll your consumer debt - credit cards, bills, vacations, cars - into your mortgage, you condemn yourself to never being free and not learning how to live within your means so you can achieve freedom.

There are four things to find out about your mortgage so you can take action to pay it off faster than you thought possible. Many people do not know these basic facts regarding their mortgage.

1. What is your interest rate and when do you renew?

The most basic fact of all is the interest rate you pay. Even half a percent can save you thousands over the life of your mortgage. You want to be looking at rates three months before renewal, and speaking to your mortgage broker or bank manager to ensure you lock in at the best time. If you are renewing with the same lender you can do so earlier **if** it is of benefit to you.

My Current Mortgage Interest Rate is	%
My renewal date (with a new interest rate!) is:	

2. According to the bank, how many years are left on your mortgage?

When you sign up for a mortgage, they ask if you want to amortize over 15-30 years - that means, if interest rates stayed the same and you never rolled debt into your mortgage, you would be mortgage-free in that time.

In the Covid years, people bought more house than they could afford, and amortisation was stretched to the maximum. Some lenders in Canada have even gone to 40 years. Private lenders do INTEREST ONLY mortgages, meant to be a short term solution for complicated situations. The borrower pays the interest and, at the end of the loan, still owes the same principal amount - so a never ending, never lowering debt if you keep signing on.

When negotiating for a renewal, you need to drop the amortisation by AT LEAST five years each time or you aren't changing the end date at all. Always try to drop by more years to advance your mortgage freedom date!

> The bank says I have _____ years and _____ months left on my mortgage.

3. How often do you pay your mortgage?

You can pay your mortgage weekly, biweekly or monthly. You can also choose accelerated weekly or biweekly, increasing the amount of each payment set out in your agreement.

Here's a hint: Accelerated Weekly is the fastest way to zero. It means that you pay a little more each week and get the benefit of the extra pay months! That is 52 payments every year, not 12 or 26. You also save immediately on interest every time you put a payment on your mortgage.

I pay my mortgage every ________________.

4. What is your payment? What portion is interest and what portion is principal payment – the amount actually going to your debt?

Many people go for the absolute lowest payment possible when they purchase too much house. This means that their payment is mostly focused on interest.

How much is my mortgage payment?	$
How much went to interest on my last payment?	$
How much went to my ACTUAL debt on my last payment?	$

Now for the magic, the loopholes, if you will. This is where you cut your time and cost drastically. You need to know how much you can pay, penalty-free, in a lump sum every year and how much your regular payments can increase.

Most mortgages allow you to pay off lump sums throughout the year, increase your payments as well as double your payments. My mortgage had a maximum 20% of the original debt per year and 20% increase in weekly payment without penalty. How much can you pay each year without penalty? Write down both the lump sum and the maximum weekly payment.

Annual Maximum Payment	$
Maximum Increase to Payment	$
Number of times I can double my payment	

NOW: What changes can you make THIS WEEK? Can you meet with the bank and pay your mortgage more frequently? If you are monthly, go bi-weekly. If you are bi-weekly, go weekly. If you are weekly, go accelerated weekly.

Remember: Your frequency goal is accelerated weekly.

Can you increase your regular payments? Even $5 per payment will make a difference! You aren't just increasing the payment, you are decreasing the interest with every payment. More importantly, however, it will start a new habit. Set a goal for the number of extra payments or the goal amount for the year you will make THIS YEAR. Write it down. In December, set a new year goal. Always push a little harder than you think you can achieve, and even if you don't hit the mark, you will do better than you would have without a stretch goal.

What changes can you make THIS WEEK?

This week, I will:

____

____

____

____

By the end of the year I will:

____

____

____

____

A trick you learned in the debt clearing portion of this book had the biggest impact on paying my mortgage, buying my Harley, renovating, travelling and more. This has helped friends do the same, and many attribute their mortgage-free status to learning this tip years ago: You gotta learn to sweep!

I hope you swept earlier, when you learned the tip. I am going to ask you to do it again now. If you prioritise this habit in your day, you will be debt free and wealthy.

Go to online banking and move everything in the first three columns over to a savings account.

$1,34**2.78**

Your account that was $1,342.78 now ends in ---0.00 ($1,340.00)

Now look at the tens column: can you move it?

$13**40.00**

If yes: GREAT! You are now sitting at $1,300. If no: can you move some? Make it $1320 or $1310. How did that feel? How much did you move today?

Round Up: What do you need to know about your Mortgage?

Get to know your mortgage:

- What is the interest rate?
- What is the renewal date?
- How often do you pay your mortgage?
- How much do you pay and how much actually goes on your mortgage?
- How many more years in this life sentence?
- How many times can you double your payment?
- How much is the minimum lump sum payment?
- Sweep your accounts daily and make a lump sum payment as often as you can.

Interest Rate	%
Renewal Date	
Frequency	
Amortisation	years
Entire Payment	$
Principal Payment	$
Interest Payment	$
Number of double up payments per year	
Minimum for a lump sum payment	
Current Mortgage Freedom Date	
Dream Mortgage Freedom Date	

What's Next

"Shoot for the moon. Even if you miss,
you'll land among the stars."
- Les Brown

One-Two Punch: Debts and Dreams

I was somchow tuned in enough to know that if all I did was pay debt and did not attend to my dreams, I would fall off that wagon hard. Thanks, Psych 101! So not every penny I earned beyond my living expenses during the Student Loan Years went to my Student Loan Bank, Scotiabank.

I made saving and debt repayment into a game. If I got a raise or picked up an extra shift, well, I didn't need that money last payday to float my life, so I made the difference count. It went to the debt and to the savings. Gifts, a bonus, a tax refund: focus on the debts and dreams! They didn't become a part of daily living expenses. It is so easy to spend more and not even appreciate the increase in lifestyle. But taking a chunk of money and intentionally putting it towards something significant? Well now. That you can appreciate. I received great satisfaction seeing my debts decrease and my savings build towards that one goal. It kept me from spending on silly things, on conveniences, on waste.

Let's take a moment and dream.

The biggest dream I had was to own a Harley before their 100-year anniversary in 2003. So I opened a savings account at TD in 2000 - not the same bank as my regular banking: this was my Harley Account. The guy at the bank knew what I was saving for. He saw me when I was mad. He saw me when I was frustrated. Instead of emotional shopping, I went to the bank and deposited money into my dream; instead of celebratory shopping, I deposited money into my dream - let your emotions lead you to your dream!

Over a year after opening the account, I showed up with a paycheque: two weeks of full-time work. He asked what Todd (my then boyfriend, now husband) had done and whether I needed an alibi! I revealed that I had just turned down a three-month extension on a government contract because I no longer wanted to work the 3-11pm shift after I worked my day shift somewhere else and still had my weekend job, not to mention the seasonal job that would begin in the fall; I was working seven days a week, the equivalent hours of 2.5 full time jobs. if I was willing to give up the contract, it followed that I did not need the paycheque. There wasn't going to be one in two weeks, so into the bank it went. I knew this would slow down debt repayment, but I was going way too hard! I picked up a few evening shifts from my other jobs, but allowed myself some evenings off. It also allowed me a little time to look for a better paying job now that I wasn't working every evening.

Fast forward November 2002 - two years after opening the account - I bought a Harley on eBay for $8,000 in time for the 2003 anniversary. And we celebrated! My best friend, Caz, threw me a baby shower. And I continued to pay my student loan. AND I committed to the couple's dream - our own home - that my boyfriend had been trying to engage me in, and the savings started up again. He had been focusing on that account, while I had eyes only for my Harley. Priorities, right? ;)

Finding the Path

Sometimes, you just can't see the path without a guide. I met Jessica Baker-Daza in 2022. She wanted to know how to pay her mortgage faster. She thought she was stuck in a house she did not even like until she upgraded in five years, or worse, retired and bought something smaller. She had a vision of the way of life she wanted to have, but just didn't know if she could have it or not; she just couldn't work out the path.

We spoke for an hour about various ways of paying her mortgage off. We went through the tips from the last section and wrote down the questions to ask her banker as she did not have all the answers. We didn't stop at the mortgage however, and during the conversation, she saw something much greater than paying off her mortgage. She saw the possibilities open up now, not years from now.

When we met the following month to go over her progress, she told me that she had put an offer in on an amazing house that would suit her future family for decades and that her old home was now on the market. "Why pay off a house I don't even like?" she asked. As we had already discussed the questions to ask, she was well-prepared for her new mortgage discussion with the bank. Her Mr. Right Now house was worth more than she imagined, and therefore building a summer kitchen in Mr. Right house was a go! She was in charge of her money and blazing a path to the life she had imagined.

Not long after, she bought a horse, something she thought was years away. It was a well-thought-out, financially viable decision. The thing about looking deeply into your finances and habits is that you can have what you truly desire and cut the rest that doesn't light you up.

It's time to dream, to discover the life you truly want, or at least find a juicy dream for the next two to five years. When my coach, Jo Bendle, Creator of the Meant for More® Method, wants to inspire my next big leap, she takes me through a visualisation exercise where I sit on a bench with ocean views and visit my next-level self. Big dreams land there, and she then gives me the support and tools to turn these dreams into reality. You can find her Bench visualisation on my website: www.mortgagelessmentor.ca/bookresources

I suggest you close your eyes, sit on the bench and dream about your future in one, three, five or ten years: the work-optional version, the worry-free version, the ready-for-anything version of you.

I want you to imagine how life will look when your debt is ***gone***. All that money eaten by interest? Those payments to repay purchases you may not even remember? That juicy mortgage payment when the house is well and truly yours? Scribble, draw, brainstorm - but dream big!! Use this space to create a vision so clear you can almost live it now.

Now that you have dreamed and plotted, write the dreams and due dates down.

Dream	Amount	Due Date	Notes

Pick one dream that lights you up, fires you up, consumes your waking moments!

THE Dream:

This is the one dream. The Harley Goal. This is the soul-saving goal.

Stay the Course, Stay the Course.... Squirrel!!!!

Did you fall off the wagon and go out with your aunt to a few consignment shops and end up with a gorgeous new wardrobe and almost brand new cowboy boots justified by the amount you just saved on all you bought? You just bought three suits, four pairs of jeans, new workout wear (do you even work out?), runners, winter boots, a new winter jacket, cowboy boots and five sexy summer dresses! But that would have been thousands new, and you only spent $450! You DESERVE something nice after all the work you do, and for the people who rely on you and....

While it is true that you deserve the crown jewels of all the royal families in the world, as you are so amazing, is that “deserving” worth keeping you in debt? So, dust yourself off, go back to the list and enjoy those boots cause you just celebrated your next four milestones. At no point, however, are you going to throw in the towel, as you DO deserve the life you are working towards. So do all those beautiful people who rely on you. And yes, you look fabulous in those dresses. I know I did!

Find the Right Advice!

A financial adviser is a person who can invest your money and take care of the management of it during threats and opportunities in the market. When looking for a financial adviser, like seeking a spouse, you have to look around. Kiss a few frogs! Find someone who speaks your language, understands your dreams, enjoys talking to you and demonstrates that they have a vested interest in you getting everything you ever wanted! Finances are a family affair! This person needs to know you, your favourite people and your wildest dreams - the ones that require financial support, at minimum.

I met my primary financial adviser in my twenties. I answered an ad regarding a financial position, and while I didn't pursue the opportunity, the company followed up offering a financial review and I accepted. Tammy Beamish and I met at a coffee shop, and we connected immediately. We talked for over an hour! There started my regular investing: $25/month.

Over the years, Tammy got to know me very well. She recognized three very important things about me, and these things changed my financial outcome.

1. I am allergic to interest and fees

2. I am better at paying off debt than I am at saving

3. I respond VERY well to a challenge

These were things I had not yet learned about myself, and she worked that knowledge to my advantage. She was the maestro; I was the instrument. One legendary move occurred after she moved from Investors Group to BMO Wealth and my portfolio did not meet the minimum household investment requirement for clientele of $100,000. She managed to flip my thoughts to see the gap between my current investments and $100,000 as a debt to myself. Well, I am very good at eliminating debt due to my aversion to interest, right? I powered up.

A good financial adviser will know your needs and help you grow your wealth. A great adviser will challenge you, support you and help you achieve more than you ever thought possible.They will know your dreams and goals and those of your family and build strategies to help you meet and even exceed those goals.

Your financial adviser needs to meet you AT LEAST once a year. If this is not happening, break up with that advisor!

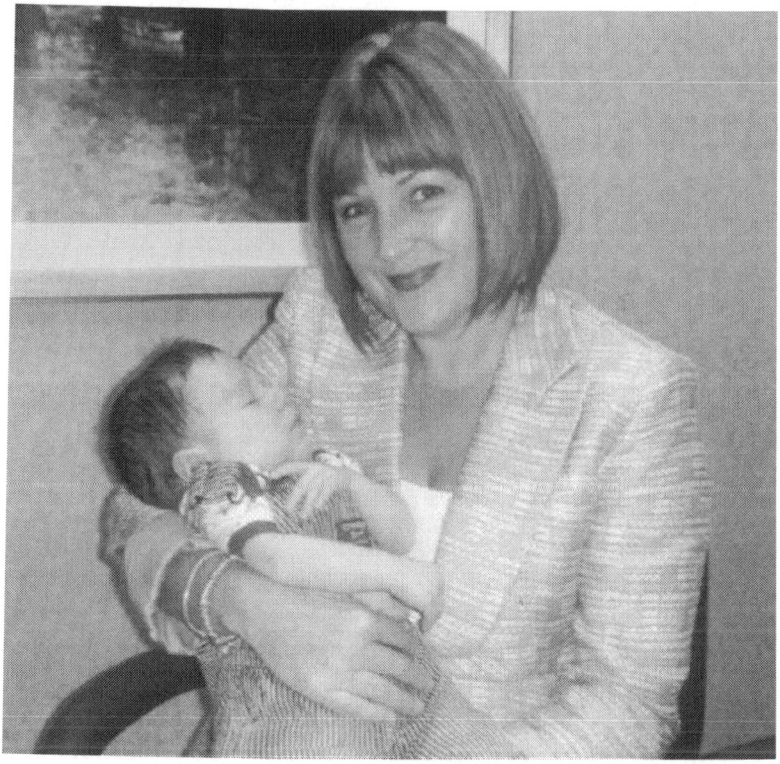

I introduced my son to Tammy when he was two months old. We opened his education fund and I started contributions immediately.

Don’t Put All Your Eggs in One Basket

You have heard the advice “Don’t put all your eggs in one basket” throughout your lives. It applies to money, too!

In addition to having Tammy in my corner with a growing investment portfolio. I have one bank with tellers available, a bank manager and financial advisers in a bricks and mortar building a drive away from my home, two online banks with no fees and another financial firm that I once worked for as a financial advisor: I had my life licence and my mutual funds licence, and intended on working towards my financial designations before refocusing on coaching. Lindsay Gilbert, my former trainer, is now helping me build investments, insure my family and play with numbers to see what changes in my future when I increase investments. Her projection software is a fun fortune-telling game as we compare my projections from 2018, when I got licensed, to now as I increase investments every chance I get. Remember: even $5 a week makes a great difference over the years.

My bricks and mortar bank had my primary mortgage and my rental property accounts for receiving rents and paying the mortgages. One online bank holds daily banking for my personal life, and the other - the one I try to forget the password to - is used to make major impacts on my lifestyle and future. I auto transfer money every payday. My taxes and my baby bonus go there to be evaluated against need and have a bigger impact on my life, instead of becoming part of my daily expenses (see Section Bonuses, Taxes and Gifts, Oh My! for more on this).

Why do I do this?

Bricks and Mortar:

Sometimes you need to walk into a bank to solve a problem. You need a bank draft, you have to pay a bill today because you forget that land taxes are due around St Patrick's Day, or you need foreign currency TODAY because you leave tomorrow, and sometimes you let a ball slip.

Another reason: anywhere you pay bank fees, you have paid for financial advice. It does not matter if you have $1 in the bank or over 1M invested: you belong to a bank therefore they provide services to you. The more you have in your portfolio of investments, mortgages, cash and credit, the more experienced the adviser, of course.

One of the best reasons to have a bricks and mortar bank is knowing the branch manager. He or she can make your life easier when you face a problem: a fee you wish to dispute or you messed up and were charged, estate questions and guidance, a free money order when you are buying a house.

My favourite interaction with my bank manager was asking him to make the final payment on my mortgage. There are two reasons I asked Stephen Bent from CIBC to make the final transfer. First, we had connected over the years and I was excited to share this moment with someone who knew what I had done to get there and had seen many a family work their way through mortgages with varying degrees of success. Second, to make sure that every penny was paid that day! Thursday, April 18, 2019 I KNOW that my mortgage was paid off, and Stephen wrote the mortgage discharge letter with joy. Do you know that if you provide a mortgage discharge letter to your insurance company, you pay less house insurance? Another financial benefit to being mortgage free.

Stephen has had my business for many years. I even followed him from his previous branch in Barrhaven to Kemptville, Ontario. He is an excellent leader, ready to celebrate, uplift and defend his team. He is a wealth of information and, simply put, a pleasure to sit and chat with. I value that relationship. This does not exist in online banking.

Action Step: I encourage each and every one of you to call your bank, make an appointment with your branch manager, and ask for a meeting with a financial adviser he or she thinks you will connect with. They know their staff. Let them get to know you! Do not be afraid to comparison shop. You can meet with a financial adviser, not like the vibe and ask for another person. You are not stuck with anyone. You are the one seeking a service they are providing. The person you work with needs to adapt to you and be someone you can enjoy talking to. You are in the power seat; interview them for the job!

Online Banking:

The purpose of my online-only, fee-free banking is to split business (Bricks and Mortar), amazing life (online #1), and life-changing potential (online #2). One online bank has daily life: paycheques in, bills out. The other has my emergency fund as well as specific accounts for lifestyle upgrades, F.U. Account (there is a section on this later) and family vacations.

The online bank world does not care how many accounts you have within your portfolio: open one for each purpose you require and name the account! Sounds odd? Well, by naming your account you are more likely to leave it for its purpose. I did have one called Leave the Hell Alone, but normally I name them for the purpose they will fulfil. If you are dreaming of a pool or a vacation or plan on having a baby or a wedding - name the account! You will put money in, see it grow, and not be so tempted to use it on a purchase other than that for which it is intended.

Picture it: accounts named Wedding of my Dreams, Dream Home, Retire at 50, Cottage by the Lake, Harley, Two Years off with Baby - do you think you might respect those accounts and the savings you worked to amass?

Try it! Brainstorm a few nicknames here, then open your bank app and rename as many as you can.

Reset Button

New Year's Eve is not the only time for setting intentions and making goals. We are presented with many opportunities every year: first of the month, month end, quarterly, Mondays, mid year, mid month, a holiday, a weekend, September ... and my favourite: The Birthday!

Time for one more trip around the sun, and time to reevaluate where you are and how far you've come. Take out a blank piece of paper or your well-thumbed journal, and think back over the last year, two years, five years: whatever you wish to review. This year (and maybe every year!!), I will look back to 2019 just so I can write Mortgage Freedom all over again! That's my favourite financial milestone!

Time to review where we are financially, physically and emotionally. Review how we spend our resources: time, money, energy, kisses. How can we make this year one that we look at as the start of something amazing?

When will you do a deep review of how far you have come and the way forward? Pick three to four times a year to review. Different seasons have us thinking differently and spending in different ways! Place the check-ins at times when you need to refocus, when extra money may flow in or out, and when you need to recommit to your beautiful, amazing goals.

January	February	March	April
May	**June**	**July**	**August**
September	**October**	**November**	**December**

In the past #____ year(s), I have "rocked it like a rocky thing"[3] in the following ways:

____

____

____

____

In the next 90 days, I plan on rocking like a rocky thing in the following areas:

Debt #1:

____

____

____

____

3 Quote by Jo Bendle, Creator of the Meant for More® Method, any time one of her clients shows up and nails it.

Dream #1:

____

____

____

Personal:

____

____

____

Ramp it up! You are good - how can you be great?

Now that you have worked through some very heavy lifting, it is time to turn to a few ways in which you can boost your impact on debts and dreams. While the Sweep is truly the super hero, there are different ways to use it and other tips and tricks that will set you on a path to achieving everything you ever wanted. As we have now mentioned the sweep, however, go and sweep your accounts. How much went to the debt? How much to the dream?

The Christmas Hangover

Once a year, right on schedule, Christmas arrives! Along with joyful memories in the making and the magic of lights, candles and mistletoe, there is a darkness lurking: The Christmas Hangover.

Like a night of too much eggnog, which is all laughter and wit, followed by a heavy, dull morning, taking longer to recover every year, the Christmas Hangover is the waking to bills from flashy presents, the sick feeling of insurmountable debt that takes months to clear. How many working hours do you need to repay the debt? And for what?

If you think back to the best gifts you have ever received, the ones you used, cherished and loved, the ones that were absolute perfection - what do they have in common? I'm guessing that the gifts that mean the most are the ones that took time and thought and searching, not the ones that cost oodles of money. Am I right?

In the moment, in front of people who gasp in delight (and jealousy), a person may feel more special receiving lavish gifts. But how much thought was put in? Anyone can throw money at a gift. Think of a gift as a thank you, an acknowledgement, a love token, a helping hand to someone in a rough spot. If we were to keep the tags on and add how long it would take to recover from purchasing gifts, would it be as appreciated? Would you be told to take it back? And if you weren't, what kind of friend is that?

We all know that the Christmas List is long when we start writing down all the names of those we know and love. Think about it. We buy gifts for friends and family, coworkers, our partner's coworkers, our children's classmates and teachers, our neighbours, acquaintances, their children... But, keep in mind that not everyone requires or deserves a gift every year.

Sit and think of the year gone by and the people who surrounded and supported you, were supported by you, made a difference in your family's life: those who are a part of your life, not just passing through. Beside each name that belongs on that list, write a few words or ideas that describe them, your relationship, topics of conversation, their big, juicy dreams. There, you will find the perfect gift!

For example, your friend wants to start a business. She is facing the criticism everyone faces when telling their inner circle, but you, amazing friend that you are, have seen the evidence that she is truly amazing and could make a go of this. You purchase the 10 Minute Superhero app gift option. You research a few tasks she needs to do to get started that can all be completed in 10 minutes or less, download a blank card, fill it in with your ideas, roll it up and put a beautiful ribbon on it. You can even fill one in for yourself with check-ins, brainstorming sessions and share-the-love days. You are not only getting her past the freeze or flight point on this exciting journey, but you are telling her that you heard her, you believe in her and you will be there every step of the way. All for under $5. If you wish to check out this magical app, you can find it on my website at www.mortgagelessmentor.ca/bookresources

The goal becomes keeping costs down without being cheap and insulting those we love, shopping sensibly and from the heart, and waking up in January clear-headed and with a solid bank account balance.

Review your finances and upcoming income and determine an amount that will not mortgage your future. Something you can either pay in cash or pay off 100% on the credit card due date.

Here are some ideas:

For groups: bake or cook with your children! Treats or spaghetti sauce on hand during the busiest visiting season of the year are invaluable! Make labels or tags for that added touch.

For teachers, support local businesses, make a donation to the school or a children's charity (literacy, perhaps?) or let your child choose on a budget. They KNOW their teachers. Don't assume teachers want to add yet another mug to the collection or give up loads of real estate on their shelves for your gift, either! Keep dustables to a minimum. One year, I went to the local charity shops and purchased Hallmark Christmas ornaments representing the subject taught or the relationship my son had with each teacher. Another year, I bought gift cards from my friend's restaurant, Salamander's in Kemptville. Win-Win: my son said "Thank you," to the teacher, and I said "I believe in you and your business" to my friend!

Secondhand is amazing! My husband likes to buy me Pandora beads. Yes, we can afford to buy new, but why? Anytime of year, he is on Kijiji or Facebook Marketplace finding the most glorious beads for my bracelet that truly capture our life at this moment: my sayings, our activities, my relationship with our son, Little Bear, which is where it all began: a bracelet, a heart and a bear. My heart was full! And so were our accounts!!

What about the Christmas Olympics, you may ask? Flashy gifts from siblings or a group Christmas where some kids are spoiled rotten and you are trying to tame the spending? Have a family conversation - a planning party amongst adults - where the rules of engagement are laid out. Explain what you are trying to achieve and see if you can get everyone on board. The focus is on the kids, the budgets are outlined and the competition is turned to who can get the best present at the best price! Go for the memory banks!

If they continue to splash the cash, know that you are building a future for your own family that is beyond wrapping paper. As Adam M. Grant, author of Hidden Potential: The Science of Achieving

Greater Things[4] says "It's more important to be good ancestors than dutiful descendants". No one else is paying your bills, and no one else is able to put your debt in your past. Your main responsibility is to your household and to your future!

Also: watch the eggnog. Moderation in all things increases enjoyment long term!

---

4 Adam M. Grant, Hidden Potential: The Science of Achieving Greater Things, Penguin Random House, 2023.

What's with the Title of This Book?

If you ask Jen Keogh, she could probably explain it for days, if not weeks. While for the past few decades, her mother-in-law, my Aunt Eva, tears down the tinsel and covers the house with balloons and cake, it wasn't always that way. Born on the 25th of December, she has heard "one big gift or two small ones" so many times she could spit! Anyone born within two paycheques of Christmas knows that line well, even though siblings who were fortunate enough to escape the Christmas zone receive a big gift for each occasion.

My sister had two children born within 12 days of Christmas - one on New Year's Eve Eve (December 30) and one on Twelfth Night (January 5). While as a child, her first born, celebrating late February, would cry to have the tree remain for his birthday too, he has since appreciated the extra celebration enjoyed outside the Christmas pay periods.

Every year, my sister was stressed! Finally, I asked: "Do you know when your children's birthdays are?" "Yes." "Do you know that Christmas falls on the same day every year?" "Yes." "Then why don't we prepare? Take a paycheque in the summer for each child, either buy the presents then or put it aside for Christmas." When that didn't happen, I suggested putting a little aside every pay for Christmas at large. Nope. Sure, she pulled off Christmas every year, and we witnessed very happy children around the Christmas tree, but her stress never ceased. Still stressed, sis?

A Coffee a Day Keeps My Dreams Away

I will start by saying anyone who tries to come between me and my coffee is either fearless or clueless. My cousin, Mandy, even bought me a fantastic shirt to serve as a warning.

Having your daily coffee at a coffee shop instead of at home, however, is a major expense. Some caffeinated pleasures are almost $10! Do a quick google of your favourite coffee shops and actually

LOOK at the price you are paying and multiply it by the number of times you went last week.

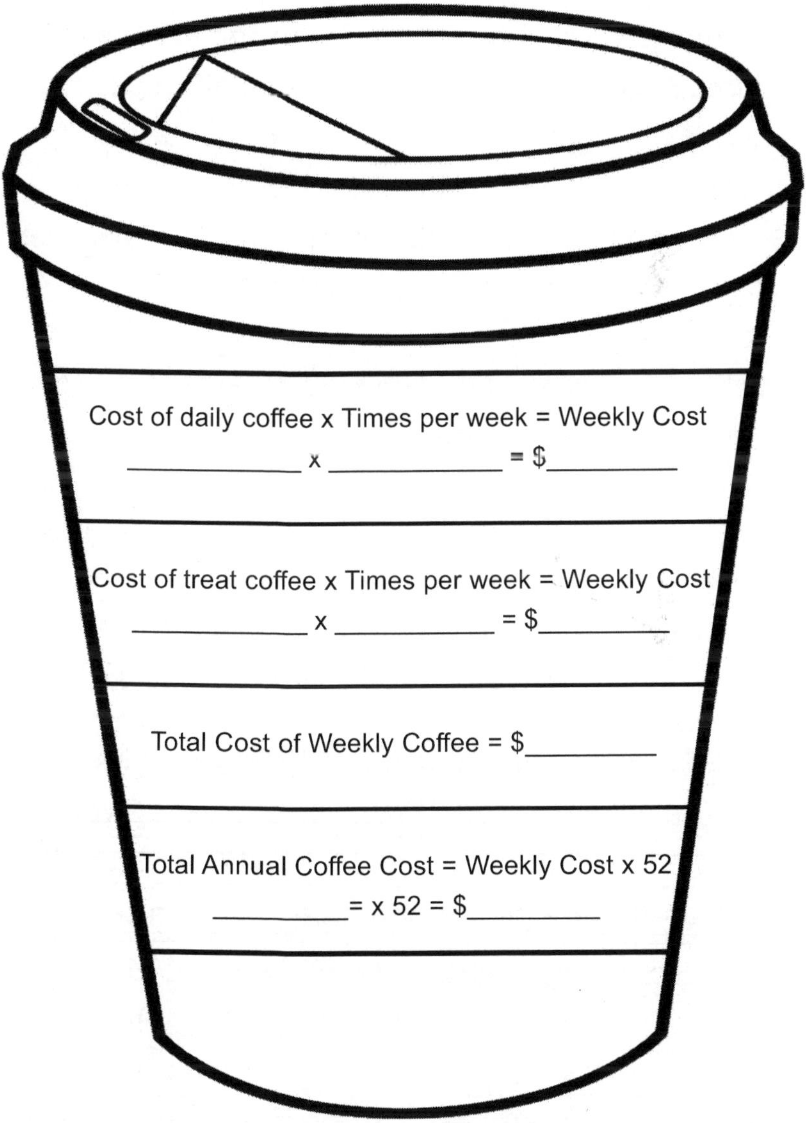

You are prioritising that coffee over vacations, children's education funds, debt freedom, mortgage freedom - whatever your next goal is. Don't cancel the coffee with your friend, the catch up, the seasonal treat - my son and I go for a Shamrock Shake every year when they come out at McDonalds - but reconsider the automatic drive-through coffee that you don't even finish. Buy a nice coffee pot and a good coffee and a travel mug! My favourite coffee, other than that one in Cuba on a farm, is Eight O'Clock Coffee, the black bag. I grind for twelve cups and set the water for 10. We call it Steel Toed Boots Coffee and it is perfect!

Before you leave the house next time, can you make coffee to go? Next time you want to hit the drive-through, take a moment to consider: Can you skip it for the sake of your debt-free dreams?

Not a coffee drinker? Don't shake your head at us! What is your treat? Wine? Cigarettes? Overdue library books? Pokemon cards? Take-out? Do the math on the things you regularly spend money on that could be sourced in a more cost effective way. See where you can save money in your daily life!

Raise Time!

You have been working hard - hopefully doing what you love! It is now time to get a raise and more vacation days. Keep in mind, a bonus is not as good as a raise - it is not a guarantee and it doesn't help your borrowing power. Vacation days, however, certainly help your family and friend connection as well as your mental wellbeing.

Back to that raise! The night before payday, you went online and split your remaining paycheque in two - half to debt, half to dream. The time will come when it is 100% to dream, or split between two spectacular dreams! You wake in the morning to a fresh new paycheque, all automated payments already gone through. Clean the account. Now look at the amount you received as a paycheque today and compare the paycheque from last time. Your lifestyle has not changed in two weeks, just your paycheque. Transfer the difference between today and last pay to the biggest impact item on your list - is that a debt or a dream? Now, make the commitment. Set an automatic transfer from your pay to your future in the same amount every pay. It is life changing! You will also need to clean the accounts again, now that you made another transfer.

The same applies with major decreases in overhead.

When we found our current home, we were living in a condo across town. We tried selling our home privately, then handed it over to a real estate agent when we realised we were soon going to be owning two homes. That year, 2008, was a bit of a financial crisis year in Canada. For us, it was an incredible year of abundance: buying the dream home, getting married, going on a honeymoon - Todd's first vacation abroad. Two mortgages were not exactly on my list! Life does, ready or not, happen. CIBC helped us get a mortgage at the 11th hour that would hold both mortgages while we searched for a buyer. That was May. In October, we were married in the backyard of our new home. Just before we hopped on a plane, our real estate agent called to say he had a buyer and that they just had to clear finances. "Don't worry. Your condo is sold!" Off we flew on our first adventure as husband and wife. A few times on the trip, when the condo came up, Todd would be so grateful that it had sold. I simply said, "I haven't seen the paperwork from our lawyer, Izzy." We did not change our plans for the honeymoon, shop more than intended nor splash cash as newlyweds with only one home might do. When we got home, we learned that the financing rules had changed while we were away and the buyers could not meet the new stress test. We still had two mortgages to pay.

In December, we finally sold the condo. To celebrate, Todd wanted to buy his first ever new vehicle, a family vehicle for our (hopefully) soon-to-arrive children: a Jeep Liberty. I sat down with the finance folk and asked how much I needed as a deposit to make the bi-weekly payments a specific number. They thought I was weird. I paid the condo mortgage weekly - the fastest way to zero! - and I wanted the Jeep payment to be no more than the condo payment had been. That way, one week was Jeep, one week was investments. I had been holding two mortgages for almost eight months. I had gotten used to it. Yes, I could have just allowed that extra money to flow into daily lives and buy more stuff, but because I was already planning before the money arrived, I was ready to direct it as soon as it was available.

Seek out opportunities, even temporary ones, to repurpose money from one regular expense to a debt or dream. Redirect the savings to something important to **you**. What about that most annoying debt? They should all be very annoying, but we all had that one... Or a dream that lights you up? My first Harley was that for me. Could be early retirement, a cottage on the lake, education fund for you or your children, leaving a job, or visiting your grandmother for her 100th birthday - in December 2024, I am on a plane for that centennial birthday bash!

Do you remember that time the world shut down? We didn't drive as much, we ate at home and we made our own coffee. Purchases were focused on family time and making our homes an oasis. Did you by any chance notice that there was more money in your account? Or were you one who signed up for Amazon Prime and helped keep the post office and other mail delivery services alive?

Think of two items on which you would like to focus found money: one debt, one dream. Write them down. You should have written them in this book in the earlier sections, but in case you jumped around and got here first, flip back to the exercise in the section "Now for a Plan!" and determine your focus. Commit. Re-commit. Eagerly seek out the first opportunity to act.

By evaluating your daily spending and differentiating between soul-enhancing activity and automatic purchase with no benefit, you can redirect the savings to things you value.

That daily coffee: now it's funding your child's education.

That tax refund: it's become your family vacation fund.

That raise: it's either the start of a down payment or helping you pay off your mortgage.

And those sneaky little purchases you used to make: now they're intentional savings for your retirement.

Buy the Best You Can Afford - Oh! A Sale!

Have you ever bought something you didn't really need just because it was on sale? And because it was on sale, you bought it in a variety of colours?

What about buying for the points on your credit card? "Oh, but I am getting points, so it's ok," you say.

My grandmother was very upset with me at high school graduation when she sent me some money to buy something and I chose gold plated earrings with fake bling. She insisted I return the earrings and buy something of high quality. "Buy the best you can afford, Rosy."

What she has done throughout her long life is buy items that stand the test of time—as she has! While she may not have expected to live past 99, she always bought high-quality items that last. Sadly, we can't expect the same from our disposable generation. Her appliances have been working for 70 years, while mine need major repairs after just five. Still, we can choose to buy items that will last as long as possible, instead of the cute thing that will only last a season before being tossed and replaced. Balancing quality and cost is an essential piece of your financial stability - knowing what you actually need is THE essential piece to controlling your spending.

Being committed to buying on sale and ahead of time - it is always more expensive when you need to buy it NOW - can be a big part of your financial wellbeing. It can also cause your financial downfall.

In our household, Todd does the cooking and the grocery shopping. He has an inability to walk away from a deal, whether it is something we knew we wanted before he saw it or not. I am more interested in putting a bit of money away in an investment, towards renovating my home or hopping on a plane than in buying 14 boxes of Cheerios and a case of Easter chocolate that was such a great deal.

With those deals comes the famous line attributed to wives all over the world: “Look how much I saved you, Honey!” I am the one concerned by the question “How much did you spend?!”

My cupboards, freezers, and shelves are overflowing with his great deals. I'm still working on getting him to understand that a deal is only great if it's something we actually need and will use!

Luckily, we pay off our credit cards every month—except for a few months over the last few years when my mental health was in serious distress, and money was the last thing on my mind. The bills stayed unopened while my mind was on fire. Thankfully, I had automatic payments set up, which kept us from being flagged for collections. We ended up paying hefty interest on our purchases, which didn't help my mental health either!

Consider what happens when you don't pay off your cards every month. You scored a great deal, put it on the card, got your precious points, and didn't pay it off for four months. At 19.9% interest, how much did you really save?

And what if you don't pay at least the minimum? Your credit score takes a hit, and just like trust in a relationship, it's easy to lose and hard to get back!

So, why not try a different method?

Know what you are focusing on this upcoming year outside of your regular day-to-day expenses. If something that you were buying anyway is on sale: jump! Be open to doing your groceries based on the regular sales that occur seasonally. Certain vegetables and meats go on sale regularly. Toilet paper, toothpaste and soap last ages - when you see a great deal, focus your efforts there that week, not on discount seasonal chocolate. Check out flyers to find the items you are seeking for gifts, renovations, decorating, enhancements to your lifestyle.

Some of you have heard my definition of the Poverty Mindset. If every time we talk, you're in a coffee shop or browsing a dollar store, you're not just spending money—you're filling a hole and keeping yourself broke. You convince yourself that a cheap, cute tea towel or a bright red plastic mixing bowl will cheer up your kitchen—and maybe even you—and of course, you *deserve* that coffee! But here's the thing: those $1 and $2 taps add up quickly. Before you know it, you've spent a surprising amount on things that don't last, and worse, they don't fill that hole. They leave you stuck in the same cycle.

When I first started making a little money—before those student loan repayment papers landed in my hands—I used to collect Harley t-shirts and buckles at flea markets. I had quite the collection! Then one day, it hit me: if I stopped buying all that stuff, I could actually save for the real thing. So I did. And by 2003, I was riding a beautiful Harley.

So, when is a deal *really* not a deal?

- Do you actually need it? (A real need, not one you're making up.)
- Did you plan on buying it?
- Can you afford it?
- Will you pay cash or pay the credit card in full by the due date?

If you answered 'no' to any of these, it's time to stop and think carefully. Now, if we're talking about those winter tires you forgot you needed, well, you're buying them anyway for safety. Get the best deal you can—even second-hand is fine—and pay it off as fast as possible. Know when you'll need new summer tires and when to replace those winter ones. This isn't a true emergency; it's just life planning.

The roller skates, though? Put them on your list, save up, and find the perfect pair!

How to Save on Sunscreen—and Why You Shouldn't

In January 2020, we celebrated paying off our mortgage with a family vacation to Panama. As part of the preparation, I went to the store for sunscreen. It was pricey, so I only bought two bottles.

Off to Panama we flew!

- **Day 1:** Sunburn. We missed a few spots on our pasty Canadian winter skin.
- **Day 2:** Slather it on. Reapply, reapply, reapply.
- **Day 3:** We realized we didn't have enough. The on-site store only had tanning lotion!
- **Day 4:** Our first excursion to Panama City turned into a sunscreen scavenger hunt. We found some—two bottles—but barely enough.
- **Day 5:** The husband was the first one kicked off sunscreen duty.
- **Day 6:** I followed. We resorted to wearing shirts over our swimsuits, and my son and I bought hats. We had 8 more days to go, barely scraping by.

Let's break it down: A bottle of my preferred sunscreen, Neutrogena, costs $25 (including taxes). Two hats, two overpriced bottles of sunscreen from a corner store, plus all the mental stress? *Ridiculously expensive.*

Fast forward to 2024: we returned to the same resort for two weeks over New Year's Eve. This time, I had 10 bottles of sunscreen packed and ready. I even wrapped a bottle for each of us and put it under the Christmas tree before we left (because why not turn essentials into gifts when you're about to embark on a fantastic trip?).

We make countless decisions every day, always doing the best we can with the information and resources we have. But let's be honest—there's often a lot of mental clutter drowning out our voice of reason. As my grandmother always said: *Buy the best you can afford at the time.*

In hindsight, when you're spending $7,000 on a vacation, an extra $250 for sunscreen is a tiny price to avoid the hassle—and the sunburns.

Best Fit, Not Best Price

The sooner you get your financial house in order, the sooner you will have resources to make better quality choices. Over the past few years, financial consideration has played a huge role as I deal with medical issues and my son's learning challenges. Because I had my financial house in order, I was fortunate enough to have options that would have been out of my reach 10 years ago: private school, private tutor, medical care after my workplace healthcare ran out and the insurance company wasn't paying... I was able to get the care and support I needed and carry the costs without affecting my family's needs and lifestyle. Mentally, emotionally, energy wise, however? Oh my. It was heavy.

If you are still in the position of choosing between physical or mental support and daily living expenses, be sure to do the exercises at the beginning of this book. Clear your debt with small, impactful changes.

Family Finance & Other Tips

"Saving is a fine thing. Especially when your parents have done it for you."
- Winston Churchill

To all you parents out there, involve your children in healthy financial habits as early as possible. This starts with providing multiple piggy banks and helping them split any money received between these banks. Engage them in conversation about various wants, needs and dreams. Plan for their education AND plan to get them out of your house one day!

Children's Education Fund

Did you know the Canadian government will contribute to your child's education if you open a registered account? It's true! There's a cap on how much they'll match, but let's be honest—free money is free money. All you have to do is open the account and start contributing. These funds are safely locked away until your child starts post-secondary education. You can even open a family account, allowing the funds to be shared between siblings if one needs less—or none at all!

As a parent eager to support my child's future, I opened an account as soon as I could. I even tried while I was pregnant, but apparently, regulations require an actual child with a Social Insurance Number! I maxed out my contributions in the first calendar year and every year since.

Here's a trick I used to get the maximum benefit from the Government grants for children's education (Registered Education Savings Plan - RESP):

Stage 1: I started by setting aside enough from each paycheque so that by the end of the year, I had the full amount in the account. The government grant was added to my account as I made contributions. In Canada, based on my financial bracket, my contribution is $96.15 per paycheque, per child.

Stage 2: I gradually increased my contributions so that I had the total amount earlier in the year, allowing me to build a buffer.

Stage 3: Eventually, I reached the point where I had the full annual contribution ready on the first business day of the year. I'd call Tammy and ask her to transfer the annual amount to the RESP, and the government would put the full grant in at once. This way, the entire amount could earn interest from January 2, instead of waiting until the end of the year to have the full contribution.

For me, the full contribution was $2,500, and the government would add $500. Depending on family income, the amount you need to contribute may be less. It might seem small, but 17 years of $3,000 contributions, plus interest, can add up to a tidy sum by the time your child heads to post-secondary. In fact, I already have more saved in my son's RESP than I spent on my entire university education (minus interest). Never underestimate the power of savings and compound interest.

If there is no grant available in your country, create your own education fund.

I also reached out to family members, kindly asking them to consider contributing to his education fund instead of buying toys or clothes. I even suggested they include a note predicting what he might become one day, based on his current interests.

My Robert-in-Law embraced this idea that first Christmas. He made a contribution for my four-month-old son, along with a card that read:

> Welcome to your 1st Christmas
>
> Since you can't read, let's just get whoever is reading this to give you 3 zuberts and a kiss on the cheek. :)
>
> Love, Uncle Robert and 3 cousins.
>
> P.S. The money's for your education—unless you break your mother's heart and don't go. If that happens, use it for Harley parts and beer.

My mother-in-law, Heather, took a different approach. She started putting away $1 a week in a tin at home. For 13 years now, that tin has been quietly filling up. Soon, she and my son will have a special day where they'll open a joint account, combining the money she's saved with what he's been putting away since he was six (but that's a story for the next section).

My original friend, Rose, knew he loved Cheerios, so for his 1st birthday, she gave him a box of Cheerios along with education money—something for today and something for the future!

Instead of giving toys that break or get forgotten, they decided to be part of something bigger—something that will last a lifetime.

Piggy Banks

When my son was 6, I set out two piggy banks for him, labelled *Short Term Savings* and *Long Term Savings*. I didn't think to go further, and in hindsight, I'm so glad I didn't!

Most of his money—earned from reading and from Nana—went straight into the short-term tin. After a little while, I sat him down.

> "Honey, I see this a lot with clients. Too much money in short-term savings, not enough in the long term. What are you saving for with your short-term tin?"
>
> "A car, Mommy."
>
> "An RC car? Hot Wheels? What kind of car?"
>
> "One I can drive when I'm big, Mommy."
>
> "Your short-term savings are for a real car? One you can't drive for ten years? Then what on earth is your long-term savings tin for?"
>
> "A house!"

I love my kid. After a good laugh—and an offer from him to buy my house with an American quarter—I explained we needed a few more tins: toys, the cat he was trying to earn, travel, car, house, charity, and one for buying gifts for Dad (Dad WAS the tin for gifts for Mom!). He made his own labels for each one, and we set them up on his dresser. Every time he got money, he'd choose which piggy banks to fill.

Project: Get Out of My Basement

According to Canadian dairy farmers, it used to be that all you needed to do to get the kids to move out was to "Stop Cooking with CHEESE!"[5] Well, life got more complicated...and more EXPENSIVE! You can serve brussel sprouts boiled to death every night, and they just can't seem to afford to leave. So, for those of you who would actually like to experience Empty Nest Syndrome, let's get a plan in place.

Starting today, open an account and put a portion of any money sent to your child in that account (or get an empty carboy and invest any loose change). Any time you think, "Man, won't it be nice to get my house back?" pop a few more dollars in. You will probably be stuffing in hundred dollar bills during the teen years...

If your child is nearing adulthood or already there, make it clear: 35% of their income should be going into savings for their next address, or you should be asking for rent so their stay in your

5 One stop cooking with cheese commercial : https://youtu.be/f5onKVpl25E?feature=shared

basement isn't too cushy. This will cut down on their 'Wants' budget!

What's more frustrating than watching someone spend recklessly with no thought for the future, while you're picking up the tab? And by the way, continuing to cover their costs is doing them a disservice. You won't always be there to foot the bill. Sooner or later, they'll have to handle their own expenses, and never again will 100% of their income be disposable, available for their every whim.

I get it. Houses are expensive!! How will they manage to save for a downpayment? Only by starting as soon as they are making money. Or with your help.

I have two plans in mind for my 13-year-old to get the ball rolling towards an empty nest one day. Plan A and Plan B, right?

Plan A: A friend, Dan Regimbal, is a contractor who lives down the road - he is my friend Trina's husband. He and I are discussing the renovations required in my two-level workshop to make it into a livable space - I have an office and Harley house in mind, but to start we can have a private living space for our son. Over the next four years, I will do renovations with that in mind, so that by the time he is of an age to live alone (or too annoying or smelly to live with) I can point into the backyard and say this much for rent, this much for catering services, this much for laundry services. It will give him independence (and us as well!) and a taste of paying the bills. Between jobs, Dan will work on the building to make it a beautiful living space. It will increase the value of my property and not be a big expense all in one season.

Plan B: If our son is accepted to a post secondary institution away from home, we are ensuring that we have a downpayment ready to buy a house in the university town of his choosing. We can hold it for four years (or more) and he can pay rent as he rents out the extra rooms to people at the school. We can choose to sell or keep it when he graduates.

Both options require me to keep our financial house in order. If I have my house in order, I have options. If I don't, there are no options. What are you doing to ensure that your financial house is in order? Write some ideas below.

Another part of the plan is encouraging him to find what he loves and to get the education he needs to be able to fund the lifestyle he wishes to be accustomed to. You can't slack in school and life and own three Lamborghinis. I reinforce to him that he needs to keep his options open, to allow possibilities in his own life.

Got to Get the Emergency Fund!

Oh, the Emergency Fund. We all know we need one. We seem to have the same attitude towards an emergency fund as we do to writing a will: if I do it, I open the door to disaster - and to needing it!! We also know that when we are prepared, we **don't** need it. Aren't we confusing beings?

So, let's take a positive attitude and get down to business.

Looking at your life, what is the next thing that could go wrong or the most expensive thing that could go? The furnace? The roof? Health? Prevention and maintenance is cheaper than curing an ailment! The dreaded car? You know, I once thought it was cool to have a boyfriend with a car....then the car ate my house fund. MORE THAN ONCE! Not cool!

Start with one target in mind, instead of the whole three to four months of expenses. You probably guessed it! Open an account on your online banking and name it positively, like "Top of the Dream Home to You" instead of Leaky Roof. Set some cash to go in automatically every pay.

Any time you read an article or see a show about someone who has a disaster occur that threatens their financial wellbeing, pop a few bucks in. It will grow. You need to be able to access it within a few days, so don't lock it in a one-year investment.

Once this account exists, you need to have a strong definition of Emergency. A vacation, a sale at the consignment shop or a great deal on a Pokemon card (looking at you, my son) are NOT emergencies. Some things, like regular maintenance and a 20-year-old car dying (not that they last that long anymore...) should be in your financial planning. But should and are are not always in the same space. As you are setting up for success, there will be hiccups.

F.U. Account

I would like to take a moment to talk to you about something Gail Vaz Oxlade calls the F.U. Account. According to my favourite money guru, while her friends are collecting lipstick, she is building her F.U. Account: “I don’t collect lipsticks or shoes or jewelry. I collect cash. I’ve long known that the greatest flexibility in life comes with money in the bank. Cold, hard cash, that’s my luxury.”[6]

People stay in relationships, jobs, rentals, towns that are unsafe, unsatisfying and utterly joyless - and money is one of the keys that locks us in those relationships! The next time you are angry with your situation, frustrated, dreaming of selling everything and moving to a deserted island - put something in your F.U. account. In time, you will have a stash that will open possibilities for you. Soul sucking job? Follow a spouse who got a dream job? Leave a spouse? Get offered a dream job that pays less? Death or illness in the family? Layoff? Surprise baby? Whatever is awaiting you in the future, you will have the cold hard cash to

---

6 Vaz Oxlade, Gail, “Money Sense”, December 20, 2012, https://www.moneysense.ca/columns/start-an-f-u-account/

support you in that transition. Your mind will be free to panic over everything else - but your finances will support your next step.

A Chinese proverb states that *"The best time to plant a tree was 20 years ago. The second-best time is now."*[7] The same goes for savings: the time to start saving is the day you receive money for the first time. The next best time is NOW. Open the account, add some freedom and be ready to take the leap!

---

7 Begley, Sharon. "The Best Time to Plant a Tree Was 20 Years Ago. No Matter." Psychology Today, 21 Apr. 2015, www.psychologytoday.com/ca/blog/joy-and-pain/201504/the-best-time-plant-tree-was-20-years-ago-no-matter. Accessed 4 Oct. 2024

An Acknowledgement, so you do not get discouraged

There are stages to financial stability that I've lived and witnessed over the years:

- You're so far in debt, you think, *What difference will one more purchase make?* And then another. And another.
- You start putting money on your line of credit and paying off your credit card from that line. You meet both due dates, right? (The classic robbing Peter to pay Paul strategy. Why are we so mean to Peter?) Something unexpected happens, and you fall back into debt. You feel like crying.
- You build a small cushion. You celebrate. You feel proud. Then something stupid happens, wiping it out. You want to scream, *What was the point?!* The point is—you didn't go into debt.
- You build a bigger cushion. You celebrate again. Something happens, but this time, you think, *Aha! That's why I have an emergency fund.* You cover the expense, still have money left, and start replenishing it. You celebrate once more.

- You finally have a lovely, plump cushion. You've planned for when things will need replacing—roof in 15 years, furnace in 12, car in 10, spouse in 20 (or sooner if they leave that wet towel on the bed one more time!). You've built up a nest egg, or several, after researching prices and inflation. You're sitting on an F.U. investment, your kids' education is fully funded, insurance policies are in place, your vacation fund grows, and you have money set aside for fun and family treats when opportunities arise. You smile and think, You've come a long way, Baby![8]

It's not an easy road, and it takes time. But if you focus your energy on the vision of freedom for yourself, your family, or even future generations, you will get there. And perhaps you can shorten the road for your children and grandchildren, or those yet to come.

---

8 Stanford University, The Stanford Research into the Impact of Tobacco Advertising (SRITA) Collection: You've Come A Long Way, Baby, https://tobacco.stanford.edu/cigarettes/womens-cigarettes/youve-come-along-way-baby/

Irregular Income

Are you in a commission-based job or working for yourself in a feast-to-famine situation?

For those of you without regular, steady income, there may need to be a whole other book written. In the meantime, know that your emergency fund is even more important as a blow to you has severe consequences; it may even mean going back to corporate to recover.

As quickly as you can, build a three-month buffer. This is the amount it takes you to keep body and soul together for those living under your roof - all essential costs when you cut away the nice-to-haves. This amount is different for everyone. If any money comes out because of a real emergency, which for you may include no payables at month's end, replace it as soon as you receive new money. Once built, the urgency level drops a bit. You will not be in the clear, however, until you have a good 6-12 months in the bank invested in an accessible way. The first three months should be easily accessed, while the rest can roll in investments and be triggered to pay out within a three month time frame, short term, low to moderate risk portfolios. Talk to an adviser to layer these investments.

Estate Planning

"Nothing is certain except death and taxes"
- Benjamin Franklin

Get a will!

So, I know you are working hard to build your life, your family memories and your assets so that you can, one day, allow the government to decide who inherits and be paid for managing your affairs, leaving your favourite people waiting for the process to be handled by someone else.

Right?

No??

Do you have a will?

A will ensures that your hard earned assets go to the people you love the most in this world. Conversations at various times in your life will ensure the maximum amount of your assets will be passed to your favourite people.

When I bought my first condo, my boyfriend (now husband) was not on title, so we asked our real estate lawyer if he could write up our wills. We wanted to ensure that this joint asset would seamlessly transition to Todd should something happen to me. Imagine my surprise when my lawyer, Izzy Farber of Farber, Robillard Leith in Ottawa, Ontario, calmly looked at my boyfriend and asked him his intentions: was he planning to marry me? Was he planning on having children with me? With my father and brother deceased, this was the first time anyone had asked his intentions!! In the will, Izzy wrote, “In contemplation of my marriage to RoseMarie Keogh” and had a provision for all of our unborn children as beneficiaries should something happen to both of us. Izzy future-proofed our will in case we never came back to adjust the details. He advises regular updates, but sadly, people ignore that advice. Once may be all he gets to protect his clients.

Why, you may ask, with a future-proofed will, would you need to change it? Simply because, when things change in our lives, we are resistant to taking the action required to protect ourselves and our loved ones, thinking we are covered.

Picture it: Your beautiful babies are running in the back garden and you have the enlightened idea to get a will and power of attorney done. Amazing! Adulting for the win.

Twenty-five years pass.

Do you have a will? Yes.

Is it appropriate? No.

Should something happen to you, it will not be your adult children in charge. It will be the person you thought suitable when your children were still running through the sprinkler. Depending on the scenario, it may work out. But what if it doesn't?

An old friend of mine lost his parents within weeks of each other, and the wills were 30-40 years old. One of his much older cousins had been named the executor instead of him, the child who had stayed behind to support them through medical issues and old age. The cousin walked in and evicted him from the only home he had ever known, paid a relative to prepare the house for sale and sold it to that same person for well below market value. That was NOT the original intent of the will. It was meant to protect their children! He and his siblings lost out and had to take the executor to court, all while dealing with deep grief.

Other reasons to make changes are to include power of attorneys medical and financial, as well as guardianship documents. But what if you have a falling out with the person who is meant to be your child's guardian? When it happened to me, I didn't want my son to be raised by someone who had grown to dislike me immensely. I had to rewrite the documents to protect my memory in my son's life should something happen before he was of age.

There are many reasons to revisit your legal documents - add it to your calendar every year. Do not rewrite on a whim, but do review on a regular basis to ensure the right people are the beneficiaries (did you want to leave it to the cheating ex?) and, depending on ages, whether or not your children are ready to be the executors as well as the beneficiaries.

A word about executors: Your executor should be, when possible, one of the beneficiaries! That person is likely to prioritise wrapping up the process and not squandering the assets. Also, there is a percentage of the estate that goes to the executor - this way, even though the task is emotionally draining and time consuming, at least the person who is to inherit also gets that portion of the estate. If there is no one you can turn to for this responsibility and your children or those who will inherit are not ready or capable to perform the duties during their period of grief, there are Trust accounts you can set up. For a small fee, you can arrange a trust that can be modified until you die, and a professional will take care of everything including final taxes and disbursements, according to your instructions. Talk to your estate lawyer and your financial adviser for recommendations on a Trust company.

I asked Izzy to provide a list of the basic questions required to create a will. With these answers ahead of the first meeting, we only require one meeting to sign the will instead of two: one to provide information and one to sign. Check with your lawyer if there are additional questions they need.

Here are the questions he provided. Answer them and compare them to what is in your will.

Wills/Power of Attorney Questionnaire

Full name(s):
Address:
Phone (home):
Phone (business):
Cell:
Email:
Citizenship:
Marital status:
Executor:
Alternate:
Disposition of household goods, personal effects, jewellry, automobiles, etc.

Will you make a non-binding memorandum or list to help your family make a fair division?
Funeral, burial and other special instructions
Residual Beneficiary
Alternate(s)
Age(s) to inherit
Guardian(s)
Do you already have a Will?
If so, where is the original?
Attorney
Alternate(s)

You know what you have to do. Don’t wait, leaving your favourite people in the lurch. Pick up the phone. Make the appointment.

A word on Insurance

Well, maybe a few.

From having no insurance to trying to make those who are left behind millionaires, people have been all over the map with how they deal with insurance.

First thing to consider: You need to own your own insurance! When the economic cycle includes "restructuring," another word for layoffs, your insurance is gone with the job. When you retire, the life insurance is no longer yours either! You do NOT want to be life insurance shopping in your retirement years!

There are two kinds of insurance available: Permanent and Term.

Consider permanent insurance as owning and term insurance as renting. The Term policy is the one you want to have and never use! As no one is getting out of here alive, however, you WILL use the permanent kind. The earlier you purchase your permanent insurance, the cheaper it is. We bought our son's permanent policy when he was eight years old and will have it paid up by the time he is 16. When he goes out into this world, his family will be protected, and he will only require the cheapest kind of insurance to handle his mortgage. You won't be falling into debt, right, my son?

When thinking of insurance, consider the permanent costs you need covered as well as the temporary.

Permanent needs, requiring permanent insurance at the youngest possible age, include:

- The cost of burial and funeral service - you can pre-pay your services, but be aware that things can change, so have a little extra put aside for the person who has to deal with it, cause, well, you won't be here! Another option is a service like Everest, a funeral concierge (ooh la la!), that will handle negotiating your final costs instead of your spouse or child being emotionally blackmailed.
- Any sum you absolutely must leave, but ask yourself why you are paying insurance to cover this.
- Death taxes! Real estate transfer taxes, anything your estate lawyer says you need. Yes, you need to talk to an estate lawyer! Mine is a

wealth of knowledge as my circumstances have changed over the 20+ years of our relationship. The advice given to me in my twenties, without assets, without a child, was very different to the advice given to me in the summer of 2023 with rentals, a child, a business and a good net worth. And of course, the money I need to have to cover the costs has gone from very little to something I have to pay attention to. Again, ask yourself why you are paying insurance for this and not putting it aside.

Temporary needs, requiring varying lengths of temporary (aka cheapest) insurance, comes in varying terms such as 5, 10, 15, 20 and 30 years. This insurance will be to cover:

- Debt, including your mortgage. I broke the mortgage in half, with half the debt covered by a Term 10 and half covered by a Term 20. Didn't end up needing the last nine years of the Term 20 policy!
- Children's education, wellbeing, prom night limo, down payment support, wedding day flowers - don't forget to write letters and leave them with someone you trust.

- Wage replacement - Note that a stay-at-home parent is providing a replacement for a paid service, so be sure that you are insured if you happen to be the domestic goddess or god.
- Spousal support that you are responsible for in a legal settlement.
- Child support for any children no longer under your care.
- Singles cruise....well, maybe that should be on the permanent needs list.

Action Step: Get a will! Ask your friends for recommendations for an estate lawyer or look into services like Everest. Just get a will.

And then sometimes, it isn't even ABOUT money!

I had a call with a potential client who is doing everything right! Sweeping, keeping business separate from personal, spending less than she makes... The issue is the conversation at the kitchen table or the pillow talk.

Let's take the emotion out!

You know by now how much it costs to run your life. Housing costs, utilities, children's education and activities, clothes, gifts, transportation, investments, savings, land taxes, income taxes, emergency fund, F.U. Fund, renovations, summer activities, vacations, stationary and books, internet, TV, cell phone, personal care, restaurants and coffee shops, groceries, time with friends (yes, that costs gas, a bottle of wine, wear and tear on your running shoes).

Now you know what it costs, and if you and your spouse make an equal amount of money, break the year up by 12, and each spouse puts 50% of the monthly amount into a joint account. If your wages are not equal, work out the correct percentage so that one spouse is not overburdened due to a much lower paycheque. What percentage of income does the lower paid spouse make? That is the percentage of the overall costs they will pay. Both spouses contribute to the account to pay everything. I am hearing more and more that one pays groceries, gifts, gas - the consumables - while the other pays mortgage, cars, renovations. What happens when the mortgage is paid? The cars are still running after the payments? The groceries and gas skyrocket? If you run on percentage, both will benefit as things are paid, and no one will be overburdened by a hike in expenses.

All bills will now come out of the joint account, eliminating the stress of how each of you spend or hoard money. Quarterly dates are recommended to ensure that you are correct in your estimates! Let technology help you and set an alert if the money in the joint account goes lower than the threshold of comfort. Put a reminder in your calendar and perhaps a little aside for a nice dinner or a bottle of bubbly while you review.

If you both know that the lifestyle you have become accustomed to is not threatened by your partner's spending, you will be less likely to get stressed out and start a fight. You can enjoy your discretionary spending in the way that fills your cup. Is that a business retreat for your passion job? Is that a weekend away with your favourite cousin? A coffee date with a friend every week to maintain your mental health? A new pair of roller skates even though you haven't been on a pair in 35 years? Mine are teal with light up wheels!

What if one spouse is a stay-at-home parent? What is the cost of the services provided? Pay the stay-at-home spouse that wage and then both pay into the house!

Money is emotional! Money is linked to security. Our partner does not think like we do - one of the reasons we fell in love! They also come with their own baggage, as do you. This may be one way in which you can take the emotion out, keep the love in and get to the desired outcome peacefully.

Melissa and Eric, parents of two young children, were hard working, careful with their money and always open to opportunities to improve the future for their family. When we met, financial discussions were hard between husband and wife, as there were unintended feelings of blame and shame on both sides. By sitting down to an open conversation where we talked frankly of the goals for the family and the path to reach them, they joined forces to achieve a common goal instead of looking at each other and blaming each other. We met monthly to chart the path, discuss options, adjust investments and recommit. It was a safe space to weigh the month's spending; decisions were made on insurance policy amounts, education funds for the children, retirement and emergency plans. After a few meetings and many laughs, Melissa and Eric both expressed that what was once a tense conversation was now something they looked forward to and treated as a date - they also had a pre-meeting with a little toast to their future and perhaps more kissing!

Happy Trails![9]

Every great adventure has a starting point. May this be yours. May you see your path differently and your goals more clearly. May you see the light at the end of the tunnel of debt and know that it is not a train. May your partner and your family encourage and support you - then join you with joyful abandon. Challenge a friend - my cousin and I raced to mortgage freedom - and make it fun. Do not fear financial planning. Embrace it and create the life you want.

I look forward to hearing what debts are going down and which dream is calling your name.

I believe you can do this. I know you deserve this!

Love,
Rosy the Mortgageless

---

9 Rodgers, Roy and Evans, Dale. "Happy Trails." RCA Victor Records, 1952. This was the last song played at Fred's in Chapeau, every night at last call. I use it in the same light: a farewell for now. May we meet again.

Need more support or encouragement? Find me at www.mortgagelessmentor.ca for additional support or to become a client!

About the Author

"I don't need an inspirational quote,
what I need is a freakin' coffee"
-Unknown

Rosy, also known as *The Mortgageless Mentor*, is on a mission to help action-takers build a rock-solid financial future while still living fully in the present. Whether it's achieving home ownership, growing savings, reaching mortgage freedom, or preparing for retirement, Rosy leads the charge with a fresh approach to money management that blends debt elimination with savings strategies.

Rosy's financial journey began at 16 when she moved out, paying bills, finishing high school, and heading off to university—where she, like many students, relied on loans to make ends meet. While living on student loans, she made some poor spending decisions, prioritising wants over needs, and found herself deep in debt. But when the bill came due after graduation, Rosy made a life-changing decision: it had taken her 4.5 years to get into debt, so she resolved that it would take her 4.5 years to get out. And she did.

Throughout that journey, Rosy didn't sacrifice her dreams. While paying off her loans, she bought a Harley, put 10% down on a condo, and purchased a piece of waterfront land from family. Since then, she has bought her dream home, secured rental properties to provide families with safe spaces to live, and achieved her most coveted goal—mortgage freedom. Along the way, she travelled solo to Ireland, celebrated Christmas at Disney with family, and supported her family in their passions, like BMX racing.

Rosy's philosophy centres on the belief that you can live fully while paying down debt and saving for the future. Her "one-two punch" method of focusing on debt and dreams simultaneously has allowed her to live a rich life while building generational wealth. She brings humour, practicality, and real-life experience to her work, inspiring others to take control of their finances and pursue their biggest dreams.

Through her speaking engagements and mentorship, Rosy empowers others to embrace financial freedom and create a legacy of wealth that echoes through the generations. Her approach is grounded in the belief that financial success is possible for everyone, no matter where they start.

Facebook: https://www.facebook.com/mortgagelessmentor

Instagram: https://www.instagram.com/rosy_the_mortgageless_mentor/

LinkedIn: https://www.linkedin.com/in/rosy-the-mortgageless-mentor-11a133b7/

Website: www.mortgagelessmentor.ca

Email: Hello@MortgagelessMentor.ca

What Readers are Saying

I am not a person who tends to read unless I have to. I am a person who really needs to have an interest. This book had me reading from start to finish. It was like I was taken on a finance adventure. My honest thought is this book should be taught or recommended for reading for grade 12 and university.

This informative book will teach you financial discipline, at least for me. One of the tactics suggested such as moving cents to a savings has started and I am on track to having a healthy saving account. Even quitting the Starbucks 2 times a week. I truly enjoyed this book. With this book I was able to change my financial goals and outlook that has affected me in a positive way!

— ***Matthew Pecar, Fire Chief/CEMC, Wasauksing Fire Department***

If you've got your hands on this book you're in for a treat. It's short, easy to read, and FULL of great money tips. But not over complicated money tips, simple things that normal people can use to create massive change. Full of clever ideas you won't have heard explained this way, plus small implementable tips that can completely change your financial situation. The daily sweep is genius. Get ready for a burst of enjoyment getting your money stuff on track and setting your Future Self up for more money the Rosy way!

— ***Jo Bendle, Creator of the Meant for More® Method***

If financial freedom scares you - and so do finances, generally - then this is the book for you. Rosy takes you through the steps in a way that will make you laugh. She will make you cry. She will help you to see things in a new way. If you really want to break the cycle of debt, she is here to take your hand. Read this book!!!

— ***Chris Gravel, Friend, sister, co-conspirator***

Financial literacy can be dry and sometimes hair pulling. Rosy brings a fresh perspective with practical tips to get you out of the debt mindset. Great way to get your butt in gear and start making strides for your financial goals.

— ***Heather Coleman Vice President, Enriched Academy Financial Literacy Company***

Round of applause for this glorious book-insightful, witty, easy to follow great concepts. This is not a book to be pushed aside. Read it, read it again, complete the activities, and implement them. They are life changing! You can hear the voice of the author as she guides us through with intention. I've had the pleasure of working alongside RoseMarie (our Author) and with her trust, and guided support we've utilized these skills. Our partnership has brought years of friendship, laughter, and most importantly security for our families. I love helping families build wealth and a legacy that will continue. Thank you Rosy, I am honored to be mentioned in Don't Put All Your Eggs in One Basket! I've never liked sweeping floors but I certainly like sweeping my money.

— ***Lindsay (Gilbert) Fletcher Insurance Agent-Life, A&S, and Investments***

This book is a true gem for anyone looking to take charge of their finances. It provides practical advice and actionable steps for effective money management, leading readers toward a more fulfilling life. The author presents financial concepts in an engaging and accessible way, making it suitable for anyone. Focusing on building a strong financial foundation, the book offers valuable strategies for getting out of debt and creating a solid savings plan. It encourages readers to shift their mindset and rethink traditional views on managing money.

I plan to buy multiple copies to share with family and friends who want to take control of their financial futures. It is an invaluable resource that will inspire them to tackle their financial challenges with confidence.

— ***Shelley A. Murdock, Author, HEALTHY & FIT FOR LIFE-THE STARTER KIT FOR WOMEN OVER 50***

A great gift for young people, starting off in life. You find a lot of valuable tips. Not just for young people it's a great read for anyone really.

— ***Nadee Fernando-O'Driscoll, Author, Labyrinth of Dreams***

Manufactured by Amazon.ca
Bolton, ON

43231173R00085